Why am I a mammal?

Greg Pyers

www.raintreepublishers.co.uk
Visit our website to find out more information about **Raintree** books.

To order:
☎ Phone 44 (0) 1865 888112
🗎 Send a fax to 44 (0) 1865 314091
🖥 Visit the Raintree Bookshop at **www.raintreepublishers.co.uk** to browse our catalogue and order online.

First published 2005 by Heinemann Library a division of Harcourt Education Australia, 18–22 Salmon Street, Port Melbourne Victoria 3207 Australia (a division of Reed International Books Australia Pty Ltd, ABN 70 001 002 357). Visit the Heinemann Library website at www.heinemannlibrary.com.au

Published in Great Britain in 2006 by Raintree, Halley Court, Jordan Hill, Oxford OX2 8EJ, part of Harcourt Education www.raintreepublishers.co.uk

 A Reed Elsevier company

© Reed International Books Australia Pty Ltd 2005

09 08 07 06 05
10 9 8 7 6 5 4 3 2 1

Editorial: Helena Newton, Carmel Heron, Diyan Leake, Adam Miller
Design: Marta White
Photo research: Copperleife, Wendy Duncan
Production: Tracey Jarrett
Illustration: Richard Morden, Mordenart

Typeset in 21/30 pt Goudy Sans Book
Pre-press by Print + Publish, Port Melbourne
Printed and bound in China by South China Printing Company Ltd

The paper used to print this book comes from sustainable resources.

National Library of Australia Cataloguing-in-Publication data:

Pyers, Greg.
    Why am I a mammal?

Includes index.
For middle primary school students.
ISBN 1 74070 269 7.

1. Mammals – Juvenile literature.
2. Tigers – India – Juvenile literature.
3. Animals – Classification. I. Title. (Series: Classifying animals). (Series: Perspectives (Port Melbourne, Vic.)).

599

Acknowledgements
The publisher would like to thank the following for permission to reproduce copyright material: APL/Corbis/© Tom Brakefield: p. **4**, /© Stuart Westmoreland: p. **13**, /© Randy Wells: p. **16**, /Terry Whittaker/Frank Lane Picture Agency: p. **23**, /© David A. Northcott: p. **24**; © Chris Brunskill/Ardea London Ltd.: p. **15**; Dinodia: p. **26**; Jean-Paul Ferrero/Auscape International: p. **19**; © David B. Fleetham /SeaPics.com: p. **27**; E A Kuttapan/Naturepl.com: pp.**18, 25**; Photolibrary.com/OSF: pp. **6, 12**, /AnimalsAnimals: pp. **9, 21**, /Peter Arnold: p. **17**; Reuters/Dennis Balibouse/Picturemedia: p. **20**; Skulls Unlimited: p. **10**; Stan Wayman/Photo Researchers, Inc.: p. **14**. All other images PhotoDisc.

Cover photograph of a Bengal tiger is reproduced with permission of APL/Corbis/© Randy Wells.

Every attempt has been made to trace and acknowledge copyright. Where an attempt has been unsuccessful, the publisher would be pleased to hear from the copyright owner so any omission or error can be rectified.

Contents

Words that are printed in bold, **like this**, are explained in the glossary on page 31.

All kinds of animals

There are millions of different kinds of animals. There are big animals and small animals. There are **furry** animals and scaly animals. Some animals swim and some animals fly. Some animals hardly move at all!

But have you noticed that with all these differences, some animals are quite similar to one another?

Wolves are furry, four-legged animals.

Sorting

We sort spoons, knives, and forks into different parts of a drawer to help us find the right one when we need it. Animals that are similar to one another can be sorted into groups. Sorting animals into different groups can help us learn about them. This sorting is called **classification**.

This chart shows one way that we can sort animals into groups. Vertebrates are animals with backbones. Invertebrates are animals without backbones. Mammals are vertebrates.

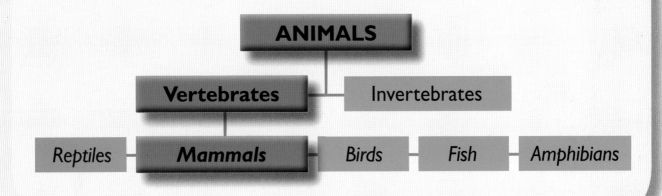

A tiger is a mammal

Mammals are one group of animals. There are more than 4000 **species**, or kinds, of mammals. Bears, monkeys, and dolphins are mammals. So are humans. But what makes a mammal a mammal? In this book, we will look closely at one mammal, the Indian tiger, to find out.

As you read through this book, you will see a ✔ next to important information that tells you what makes a mammal a mammal.

Most Indian tigers are orange with black stripes.

Different tigers

There are several kinds of tigers. They live in different parts of Asia. The smallest is the Sumatran tiger. The largest is the Siberian tiger. Both of these tigers are very rare. The Indian tiger is also rare. There may only be 3000 Indian tigers living in the wild.

Indian tiger

A full-grown **adult** Indian tiger may weigh 250 kilograms (550 pounds). This is about the same weight as three average-sized men.

An Indian tiger may be 3 metres (9.8 feet) long from the tip of its nose to the end of its tail.

A tiger's body

An Indian tiger's body is like a cat's body, only much, much bigger. It is long and thin and ends with a long tail. An Indian tiger has four thick, powerful legs. Its head is quite round, with a short **snout** and long, white whiskers. Whiskers are thick, stiff hairs that help the tiger to feel its way in the dark. The hairs on the rest of its body are soft. Most mammals have hair.

FAST FACT

Most mammals have four limbs. Whales and dolphins only have front limbs, called flippers.

An Indian tiger's head is very cat-like.

whiskers

8

Paws and claws

Like a cat, an Indian tiger has four feet, called paws. The paws have pads underneath. These help the tiger walk silently over the ground. Inside each paw are sharp claws. The claws are usually hidden away inside the paws. This keeps the claws sharp.

Stripes

When you think of a tiger, do you think of black stripes on an orange background? Most Indian tigers have this colour and pattern. But a very, very small number of Indian tigers are white, with black stripes.

These white Indian tigers live in a zoo in Ohio, in the United States.

Inside an Indian tiger is a skeleton. The skeleton is made of more than 200 bones joined together. ✔ All mammals have a skeleton inside their body.

Backbone

Running along an Indian tiger's back is a backbone. ✔ All mammals have a backbone. The backbone is actually made up of many small bones joined together. The backbone is very important because the tiger's leg bones, tail bones, **skull**, and ribs are attached to it.

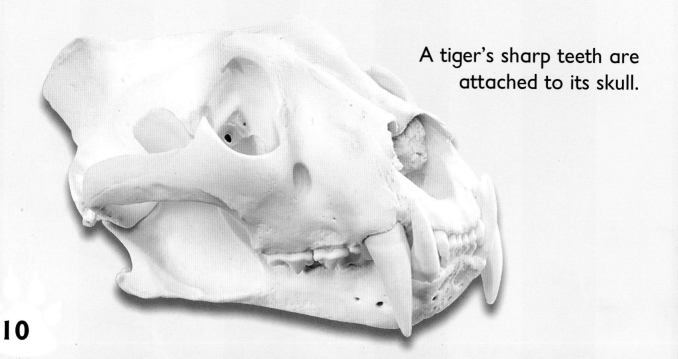

A tiger's sharp teeth are attached to its skull.

Organs

Inside its body are a tiger's heart, liver, stomach, and **lungs**. These **organs** have important jobs to do.

Breathing

The lungs take in **oxygen** from the air. When an Indian tiger breathes through its nose or mouth, air moves into its lungs. From there, oxygen passes into the blood.

✓ All mammals have lungs and breathe air.

FAST FACT

A whale is a mammal that breathes air into its lungs through a hole in the top of its body. This hole is called a blowhole.

These are some of the organs inside an Indian tiger.

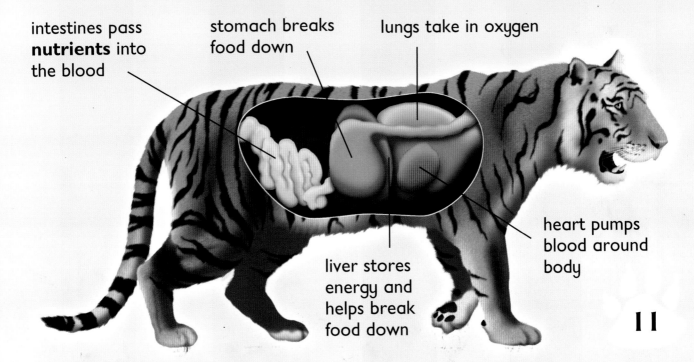

intestines pass **nutrients** into the blood

stomach breaks food down

lungs take in oxygen

liver stores energy and helps break food down

heart pumps blood around body

A warm body

An Indian tiger has a warm body. It needs a warm body so that it can do all the things it needs to do, such as hunt. ✓ All mammals have warm bodies, so they are often called warm-blooded animals.

Fur covers an Indian tiger's skin to help keep it warm.

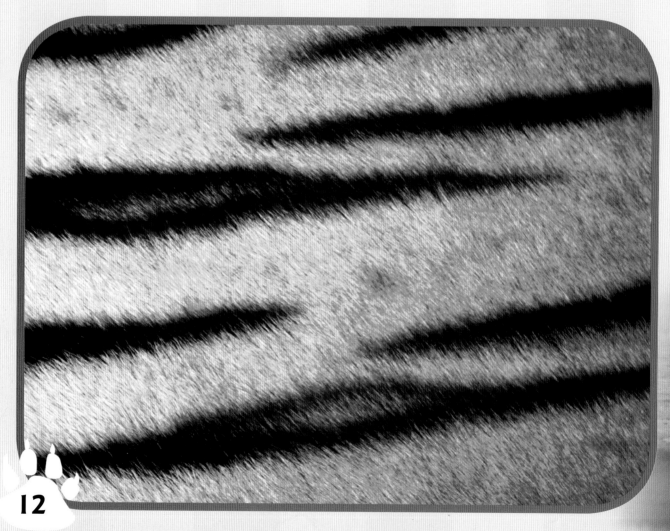

Hair and fur

Tigers have **fur** to keep them warm. Fur is thick hair that covers the tiger's body. Fur traps warm air next to the tiger's skin. Because Indian tigers live in a hot **climate**, they have short fur. Siberian tigers live in a cold climate. Their fur is long. Long fur traps more warm air.

On a very hot day, an Indian tiger cools down by lying in water. This keeps its body from getting too hot.

FAST FACT

A dolphin is a mammal that lives its whole life in water. It has no hair. To trap its body heat, a dolphin has a layer of fat, called blubber, just beneath its skin.

Food

Indian tigers are carnivores. This means they eat other animals. These other animals are the tiger's **prey**. An Indian tiger's prey includes deer, antelopes, and water buffalo.

Stalking

An Indian tiger creeps up on its prey. This is called **stalking**. When the tiger is close enough, it charges. Over a short distance, it can reach a speed of 60 kilometres an hour (37 miles an hour). But like all cats, it gets tired quickly. The tiger must make a quick catch or its prey will escape.

The tiger's stripes are good camouflage. They make it hard to see in the long grass.

Catching and killing

An Indian tiger leaps onto its prey and grasps it with its claws. The tiger brings its prey to the ground. A single bite from the tiger's four long canine teeth is usually enough to break a deer's neck.

After a big meal of 20 kilograms (44 pounds) or more of meat, the tiger may not need to hunt again for several days.

An Indian tiger hunts sambars, which are a type of deer.

15

Communication

Indian tigers spend most of their lives alone, but they use smells and sounds to **communicate** with one another. Each male tiger has a territory. This is an area of land that may be 50 square kilometres (19 square miles) in size. To let other males know this territory is his, a male Indian tiger marks the edge of his territory by spraying trees with urine. Other males smell the urine and stay away.

A male Indian tiger will roar to let other males know he is there.

Mating time

When she is ready to **mate**, a female Indian tiger makes growling sounds. She also gives off a scent, or smell. These growling sounds and scent make males come to her. Face to face, the male and female tigers communicate with more growls, hisses, and snarls. After this, they may rub their bodies together to show that they are relaxed and ready to mate.

Male and female Indian tigers communicate with one another before mating.

FAST FACT

African elephants are mammals that communicate with each other by making a low growl that can travel many kilometres.

17

Pregnancy and babies

After **mating**, male and female Indian tigers go their separate ways. The female is now pregnant. This means that baby tigers have begun to grow inside her uterus. The uterus is an **organ** inside the mother. For a while, the developing **cubs** look more like pink jelly beans than tigers. At this stage, they are called **embryos**.

A pregnant female Indian tiger cools down by lying in water.

FAST FACT

Echidnas and platypuses are the only mammals that lay eggs. These mammals are called **monotremes**.

Growing embryos

The embryos are warm inside the uterus. They take in **nutrients** and **oxygen** from their mother's blood. The embryos need nutrients to grow. Nutrients come from the mother's food. After about 105 days, the tiger babies are ready to be born.

Marsupials

Marsupials, such as kangaroos, quolls, and opossums, are mammals that give birth when their babies are still embryos. The embryos start growing in their mother's uterus but finish growing inside her pouch.

A kangaroo embryo climbs up its mother's fur to her pouch.

Cubs

The female Indian tiger finds a safe place among the grasses and shrubs of the forest undergrowth. There she gives birth to her babies, called **cubs**. She may have two to five cubs. The cubs weigh between 1 and 1.5 kilograms (2.2 and 3.3 pounds). The cubs would not be able to survive without their mother's protection.

Newborn Indian tiger cubs are covered in hair but their eyes are closed.

Taking care of her cubs

The mother Indian tiger licks her cubs clean and dry. She lies down to let them suckle milk from her **teats**.

✔ All mammal mothers feed milk to their young. Soon, the mother tiger will leave to hunt for food. She needs the food to stay alive. She also needs food so that her body can make more milk for her cubs. The cubs are too small to come with her, so she leaves them hidden in thick grass or bushes.

FAST FACT

Many mammal mothers, such as foxes, echidnas, and warthogs, leave their young in burrows or hollow logs when they go looking for food.

The mother Indian tiger carries a cub in her mouth to hide it before she goes hunting.

Mother's milk

The first food for an Indian tiger **cub** is milk from its mother. ✔ All mammal babies drink milk from their mothers. The mother tiger's milk is made in **mammary glands**. These lie just beneath the skin on her belly. When she has cubs, the mother tiger's **teats** become large and poke out through her **fur**. The cubs suck on these teats and the milk flows into their mouths.

An Indian tiger mother has four teats, but she may have up to five cubs.

What's in milk?

Milk is mainly water, but it has many important **nutrients** in it. One nutrient is calcium, which makes bones strong. Milk has sugar and fat, used for energy. It also has protein, which makes muscles grow. For the first few days after birth, mammal milk has antibodies in it. Antibodies destroy germs that might make a young mammal ill.

FAST FACT

A blue whale calf drinks 600 litres (132 gallons) of milk a day. This is enough to fill four bathtubs. Whale milk is fatty, so the calf puts on weight quickly. It needs fat to grow blubber beneath its skin, to keep it warm.

Drinking their mother's milk helps Indian tiger cubs to grow and get stronger.

Growing up

When the Indian tiger **cubs** are 2 weeks old, their eyes open. They play, wrestle, and chase one another. This helps them to learn skills they will need when they have to live by themselves. For now, their mother feeds and protects them from **predators**, such as leopards. **Adult** male tigers also often kill cubs.

An Indian tiger cub begins to explore its surroundings when it is a few weeks old.

Learning

When the cubs are 6 or 7 months old, they have begun to follow their mother when she goes hunting. By watching her, they learn how to **stalk prey**, chase it, and kill it. They have stopped drinking milk. They have grown their adult teeth, which they will use to kill and eat prey.

Indian tiger cubs leave their mother's territory, or area of land, when they are between 18 months and 3 years old. An Indian tiger may live for 15 years in the wild.

The mother Indian tiger teaches her cubs hunting skills.

Is it a mammal?

An Indian tiger is a mammal, because:

- ✔ it has a backbone
- ✔ it has **lungs** and breathes air
- ✔ it has a warm body
- ✔ it drinks milk from its mother when it is very young.

An Indian tiger is a mammal.

Test yourself: dugong

The dugong lives in shallow waters along the coasts of Australia, Africa, and Asia. It dives to the sea floor to feed on seagrasses. Every 10 minutes or so, it comes to the surface to breathe air into its lungs. Beneath its skin is a layer of blubber, which keeps it warm. The dugong has a backbone.

A female dugong gives birth each year to a calf, which swims close to its mother to stay safe from sharks. The calf drinks milk from its mother's **teats**.

Is the dugong a mammal? You decide.
(You will find the answer at the bottom of page 30.)

The dugong's skin is smooth and hairless.

Animal groups

This table shows the main features of the animals in each animal group.

Mammals	Birds	Reptiles
backbone	backbone	backbone
skeleton inside body	skeleton inside body	skeleton inside body
most have four limbs	four limbs	most have four limbs
breathe air with **lungs**	breathe air with lungs	breathe air with lungs
most have hair or **fur**	all have feathers	all have scales
most born live; three **species** hatch from eggs; females' bodies make milk to feed young	all hatch from eggs with hard shells	many hatch from eggs with leathery shells; many born live
steady warm body **temperature**	steady warm body temperature	changing body temperature

Fish	Amphibians	Insects
backbone	backbone	no backbone
skeleton inside body	skeleton inside body	exoskeleton outside body
most have fins	most have four limbs	six legs
all have gills	gills during first stage; **adults** breathe air with lungs	breathe air but have no lungs
most have scales	no feathers, scales, or hair	many have some hair
most hatch from eggs; some born live	all hatch from eggs without shells	many hatch from eggs; many born live
changing body temperature	changing body temperature	changing body temperature

Find out for yourself

Seeing an Indian tiger in the wild is something few people ever experience. Your best chance of seeing a tiger is to visit a zoo. If you have a pet cat, you could observe it to see what it has in common with a tiger. What makes your pet cat a mammal?

For more information about tigers and other mammals, you can read more books and look on the Internet.

Books to read

Bulletpoints: Mammals, Duncan Brewer (Miles Kelly Publishing, 2003)

Variety of Life: Mammals, Joy Richardson (Franklin Watts, 2003)

What's the Difference? Mammals, Stephen Savage (Hodder Children's Books, 2002)

Using the Internet

You can explore the Internet to find out more about mammals. An adult can help you use a search engine. Type in a keyword such as "mammals", or the name of a particular mammal species.

Answer to "Test yourself" question:
A dugong is a mammal.

Glossary

adult grown-up

classification sorting things into groups

climate type of weather in a place

communicate send and receive information

cub young tiger

embryo very early stage in the growth of a cub inside its mother

fur hair that grows thickly

lungs organs that take in air

mammary glands organs beneath a female mammal's skin that make milk

marsupial mammal whose young grows mainly inside its mother's pouch

mate come together to make new animals

monotreme mammal that hatches from an egg, including the echidna and platypus

nutrient part of food that an animal needs to survive

organ part of an animal's body that has a certain task or tasks

oxygen gas that living things need to survive

predator animal that kills and eats other animals

prey animals that are eaten by other animals

skull all the bones of an animal's head

snout part of an animal's head that points forward, including the nose and mouth

species kind of animal

stalk creep up close to prey

teat part of a female mammal that young mammals suck on to get milk

temperature how warm or cold something is

Index

Titles in the **Classifying Animals** series are:

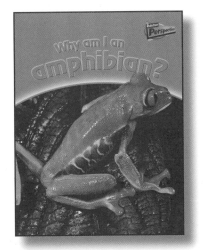

ISBN   1 74070 271 9

ISBN   1 74070 273 5

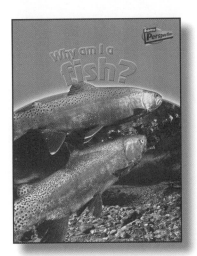

ISBN   1 74070 268 9

ISBN   1 74070 270 0

ISBN   1 74070 269 7

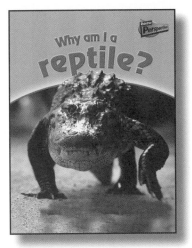

ISBN   1 74070 272 7

Find out about the other titles in this series on our website www.raintreepublishers.co.uk